# HOT Drinks

Take a cup
and drink it up!

—anonymous rhyme

# HOT *Drinks*

## COCOAS, TODDIES, PUNCHES & GROGS

Suzanne Kotz

and

Ed Marquand

Warner ⓦ Treasures™

Published by Warner Books
A Time Warner Company

CUPS *of* COMFORT

Warner Treasures is a trademark of Warner Books, Inc.
1271 Avenue of the Americas
New York, NY 10020

 A Time Warner Company

*Text by Suzanne Kotz*
*Book design and photography by Ed Marquand*
*Many of the cups used in photographs were provided by*
*Laguna Art Pottery, Seattle*

Printed in Hong Kong
First Printing: March 1996
10 9 8 7 6 5 4 3 2 1
ISBN: 0-446-91139-9

# Contents

# Introduction

Who cannot remember cupping their hands around a mug of hot cocoa before bedtime? The gentle mist of steam rising from a delicious mocha? Or the heady fragrance of cinnamon wafting from a mulled cider? Savoring a hot drink is a pleasure indeed—whether in a solitary moment of blissful quietude or in the company and good cheer of friends and family.

In this little book, you'll discover many quick and easy ways to prepare "cups of comfort" from just a few ingredients. The recipes, by and large, do not rely on "instant" products. In a world in which leisure time is a rare commodity, the simple act of making a hot drink from scratch can provide a much-needed moment of contemplation. Sipping a hot drink slows us down long enough to rekindle waning energy, relax fatigued muscles, or chase away the blahs.

Hot drinks are also a congenial addition to parties and informal gatherings. Easy to prepare for a crowd, punches and mulled drinks simmering over a low flame help create a convivial, friendly atmosphere.

These simple beverages can become part of personal or family rituals—the warm punch served every Thanksgiving, the hot toddy guaranteed to quell any cold. However you decide to enjoy these small luxuries, don't hesitate to raise your cup in good cheer to this simple treat that gives so much.

# Hot Drink Basics

## SERVING

Serve hot drinks from a warmed punch bowl, right from a pot on the stove, or in a heated mug. If serving a crowd, run your mugs through the dry cycle on your dishwasher, and hold them there until needed. For single servings, briefly submerge a mug in hot water, dry it, then fill with hot beverage.

## GARNISHES

**Cocoas and hot chocolates:** miniature marshmallows, whipped cream, shaved chocolate, grated nutmeg or ground cinnamon

**Mulled ciders and wines:** thin slices of lemon or lime, raisins or almonds, grated nutmeg or ground cinnamon

**Steamed and flavored milk:** grated nutmeg or ground cinnamon, shaved chocolate, orange or lemon zest

**Wassails and punches:** lemon slices studded with cloves, cinnamon stick stirrers, orange peel slivers, raisins or almonds

**Toddies and grogs:** lemon twists, grated nutmeg or ground cinnamon, orange slices, fresh mint

## SCALDING MILK

Choose a heavy saucepan and use low heat. Milk is considered scalded at 180 degrees F, but you won't need a thermometer. A foolproof visual clue is the formation of tiny bubbles around the edge of the pan. The bubbles can quickly turn to a scorching boil, so watch the pan carefully.

## STEAMING MILK

If you have an espresso machine, use the steam tube attachment. Fill a deep, narrow pan or beaker halfway with milk. Fill compartment of espresso machine with water according to manufacturer's instructions; be sure steam tube is closed as water heats. When pressure builds up, place tip of steam tube about halfway down into milk; open steam valve. Let steam aerate the milk for about a minute. To make foam, bring the tube tip up to the surface of the milk.

An inexpensive alternative is a cork and tube device that fits a whistling tea kettle. Fill the tea kettle half full with water; insert the cork and tube device in its spout. Heat the kettle until water boils, then position the tube tip just below the surface of the milk. Steam for about a minute.

(Pressurized steam can be dangerous; follow manufacturer's instructions and never leave steam devices unattended.)

## ALCOHOL IN HOT DRINKS

In mulled drinks that require boiling to concentrate flavors, alcohol, if an ingredient, will begin to evaporate at about 172 degrees F. If you wish, replace the lost alcohol by adding a bit of brandy or another liqueur before serving.

Cocoas
and Hot
Chocolates

# Easy Cocoa Plus

1 heaping tablespoon powdered,
unsweetened cocoa

2 teaspoons sugar

2 tablespoons half-and-half

1 cup milk

Combine cocoa and sugar in a mug; stir in half-and-half
to form a smooth paste. Gently heat milk, then
slowly stir into cocoa mixture.

(1 serving)

# Mint Chocolate

2 ounces unsweetened chocolate

4 tablespoons water

2 cups milk

3 tablespoons mint syrup or crème de menthe

Put chocolate squares in a pan; add water and melt, stirring occasionally, over low heat. Scald milk over medium heat in a second pan, then slowly whisk it into chocolate. Add mint syrup or crème de menthe and whisk again.

(2 servings)

# Honey Cocoa

1 cinnamon stick

4 cups milk

¼ cup powdered, unsweetened cocoa

¼ cup honey

Scald the milk with the cinnamon stick over medium-low heat. Remove from heat. Discard the cinnamon stick. Place cocoa in a small bowl and dribble in ½ cup milk, stirring constantly. Add the cocoa mixture to the milk and warm over low heat. Stir in the honey and heat through.

(4 servings)

# Irish Chocolate

½ cup powdered, unsweetened cocoa

½ cup sugar

½ cup water

2¼ cups milk

¾ cup half-and-half

½ cup Baileys Irish Cream

Combine cocoa and sugar in a saucepan. Place over low heat and whisk in water until a smooth paste forms. In another pan, scald the milk and half-and-half over medium heat; slowly stir into cocoa mixture. Heat for a minute or two. Remove from heat and add Baileys.

(4 servings)

# Chocolate Deluxe

3¼ cups milk

¾ cup heavy cream

1½ teaspoons vanilla

**6 ounces bittersweet chocolate**

Combine milk, cream, and vanilla in a saucepan and scald over medium-low heat. Finely chop the chocolate and combine it in a bowl with about ¾ cup of the warmed milk mixture; whisk until chocolate is smooth and melted. Add the chocolate mixture to the remaining milk and simmer, whisking, until thoroughly heated, about 2 minutes.

(4 servings)

# Mexican Hot Chocolate

4 cups milk

5 ounces semisweet chocolate

3 cinnamon sticks

1 teaspoon vanilla

Combine milk, chocolate, and cinnamon sticks in a saucepan. Stir over medium-low heat until chocolate melts. Remove from heat and discard cinnamon sticks. Stir in vanilla, then beat vigorously with a rotary beater or wire whisk until frothy (or use a blender).

(4 servings)

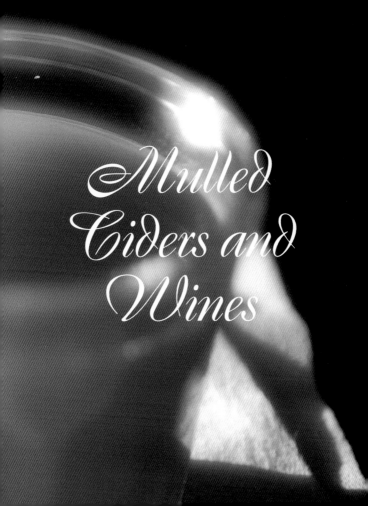

Mulled
Ciders and
Wines

# Mulled Wine

1 bottle dry red wine

2 tablespoons sugar

2 cinnamon sticks

6 whole cloves

1 tablespoon grated lemon peel

2 tablespoons cognac or rum

Combine wine and sugar in a large saucepan. Add
cinnamon, cloves, and lemon peel. Heat, without
boiling, to dissolve the sugar. Remove from heat
and add cognac or rum. Let mixture sit for
10 minutes to infuse flavors. Strain into
mugs and serve.

(4–6 servings)

# Hot Buttered Cider

1 quart apple cider

2 tablespoons brown sugar

4 tablespoons butter

Place all ingredients in a large saucepan over medium heat; bring to a simmer, stirring to dissolve sugar.

(4 servings)

# Mulled Apple Cider

2 quarts apple cider

1 quart ginger ale

juice of 2 lemons

1 cup diced dried apples

½ cup brown sugar

½ teaspoon allspice

1 teaspoon whole cloves

2 cinnamon sticks

¼ teaspoon nutmeg

Combine all ingredients in a large saucepan and bring
to a boil. Reduce heat and simmer for 15 minutes,
stirring occasionally. Remove from heat. Strain
into a warmed punch bowl and serve. For a
spiked version, add 1 cup Calvados or
applejack to punch bowl.

(12 servings)

# *Lemon Cider*

1 quart apple cider

juice of 2 lemons

4 tablespoons sugar

lemon peel for garnish

Pour cider and lemon juice into a large saucepan over medium heat. Add sugar, stirring occasionally until dissolved. Garnish with lemon peel.

(4 servings)

# Steamed and Flavored Milk

# Almond Milk

1 quart milk

4 cinnamon sticks

8 teaspoons almond syrup or amaretto

Scald milk over medium heat in a heavy saucepan. Place
a cinnamon stick and 2 teaspoons almond syrup or
amaretto in each of four mugs. Divide the milk
among the mugs and stir to mix.

(4 servings)

# Maple Milk

1 cup milk

2 tablespoons maple syrup

dab of butter

ground cinnamon

Scald the milk over medium heat. Remove from
heat and stir in syrup and butter.
Sprinkle cinnamon over top.

(1 serving)

# Spicy Milk Punch

2 cups water

¼ cup whole cloves

1 tablespoon ground cinnamon

½ cup sugar

2 quarts milk

In a saucepan, mix water, cloves, cinnamon, and sugar.
Simmer 15 minutes, stirring occasionally, and strain.
Heat the milk in another saucepan. Remove
from heat and stir in the strained syrup.

(8 servings)

# Rum Soother

1 cup milk

2 ounces rum

1 teaspoon sugar

Scald the milk over medium heat. Remove from heat. Add rum and sugar and stir to mix.

(1 serving)


# Mock Rum Soother

1 cup milk

1 teaspoon sugar

¼ teaspoon almond extract

¼ teaspoon rum flavoring

Scald the milk over medium heat. Remove from heat. Add remaining ingredients and stir to mix.

(1 serving)

# Butterscotch Steamer

2 quarts milk

¼ cup butter

½ cup dark brown sugar

Scald the milk over medium heat. Remove from heat.
Stir in butter and brown sugar until blended.

(8 servings)

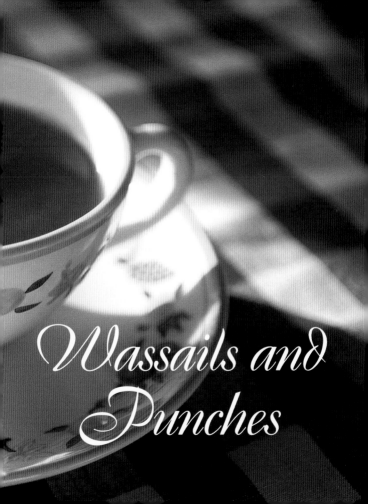

# Wassails and Punches

# Hot Apricot Punch

1 quart apricot nectar

1 cup orange juice

¼ cup brown sugar

2 cinnamon sticks, crumbled

4 whole cloves

2 tablespoons lemon juice

Combine apricot nectar, orange juice, and brown sugar in a saucepan. Bring to a boil, then reduce to a simmer, stirring to dissolve sugar. Add cinnamon, cloves, and lemon juice. Simmer for 5 minutes, strain, and serve.

(6 servings)

# Wassail

2 oranges

½ cup whole cloves

2 quarts apple cider

1 teaspoon ground cinnamon

½ teaspoon ground ginger

¼ teaspoon grated nutmeg

½ cup lemon juice

Preheat oven to 350 degrees. Stud oranges with cloves spaced about ¼ inch apart. Place oranges in a shallow pan and bake for 30 minutes. Place cider and spices in a saucepan and bring to a boil. Reduce heat and simmer for 15 minutes. Remove from heat and stir in lemon juice. Pierce the oranges in several places with a pick or fork and add to the cider.

(8–10 servings)

# Spiced Fruit Punch

2 cups water

¼ teaspoon grated nutmeg

1 teaspoon whole cloves

1 teaspoon coriander seed

2 cinnamon sticks

1 quart cranberry juice

1 cup pineapple juice

2 cups grapefruit juice

Combine water and spices in a large saucepan and bring to a boil. Reduce to a simmer and heat for 15 minutes. Add the juices and return mixture to a boil. Remove from heat. Strain and serve.

(10 servings)

# Cranberry-Pear Punch

2 cups sliced peeled pears

2 tablespoons sugar

¼ teaspoon ground cinnamon

I quart cranberry juice

I tablespoon lemon juice

Place pears in a large saucepan and mix in sugar and
cinnamon. Heat over medium heat, stirring occasionally, until sugar melts and pears are glazed.
Add juices and bring to a simmer. To serve,
place a few pear slices in each mug
before adding punch.

(6 servings)

# Apple-Lemon Punch

1 lemon, cut into six sections

6 whole cloves

1 cup lemon juice

¼ cup brown sugar

1 quart water

1 quart apple juice

Stud each lemon section with a clove. Mix the lemon juice and brown sugar in a small bowl. Bring the water and apple juice to a boil in a large saucepan. Remove from heat. Add the lemon juice mixture and the lemon slices to the hot apple juice. Cover and let mixture steep for 10 to 15 minutes, then serve.

(8–10 servings)

# Spicy Orange Punch

1 quart orange juice

1 cup sugar

3 cinnamon sticks

10 whole cloves

2 tablespoons grated orange peel

Combine all ingredients in a large saucepan and bring to a boil, stirring to dissolve the sugar. Reduce heat and simmer for 5 minutes. Strain and serve.

(4–6 servings)

Toddies and
Grogs

# Classic Toddy

1 teaspoon sugar

1 cinnamon stick

1 jigger whisky, rum, or brandy, or to taste

1½ cups boiling water

2 lemon slices

Combine sugar, cinnamon stick, and liquor in a heated mug or heat-resistant glass. Fill with boiling water. Rub the lip of the mug with a lemon slice and discard. Garnish with another slice.

(1 serving)

# Hot Buttered Rum

1 teaspoon crushed maple sugar or maple syrup

1 lemon slice

1 cinnamon stick

1 jigger rum, or to taste

1½ cups boiling water

1 tablespoon butter

Put maple sugar, lemon, and cinnamon stick into a heated mug or heat-resistant glass. Add rum, and fill mug with boiling water. Add butter and stir well with the cinnamon stick.

(1 serving)

# Gérard's Grog

1½ cups boiling water

juice of 1 lemon

1 jigger rum, or to taste

honey to taste

Combine water, lemon juice, and rum in a heated mug or heat-resistant glass. Add honey to taste and stir well.

(1 serving)

# Warm White Russian

2½ cups brewed coffee

½ cup heavy cream

½ cup coffee-flavored liqueur

¼ cup vodka

whipped cream for garnish

Combine coffee, cream, coffee liqueur, and vodka in a saucepan. Simmer until hot. Divide mixture among heated mugs and garnish with whipped cream.

(4 servings)

# Bourbon Lemonade

1½ cups lemon juice

1 cup sugar

2 cups water

¾ cup bourbon

lemon slices for garnish

Stir together the lemon juice, sugar, and water in a
saucepan. Simmer and stir until sugar dissolves.
Add the bourbon. Divide mixture among
heated mugs and garnish with
lemon slices.

(4 servings)

# Lights Out Grog

1 jigger vodka

1 jigger cognac

2 jiggers light rum

¼ cup orange juice

1 cup boiling water

1 teaspoon sugar

Combine vodka, cognac, rum, and orange juice in a heated mug or heat-resistant glass. Fill mug with boiling water and stir in the sugar.

(1 serving)